Cape Breton Island,Nova Scotia; 2024 travel guide to Canada

By: Stephen Tillery

Table of Contents

Introduction

Chapter 1: Getting Started

Chapter 2: Exploring Regions

Chapter 3: Outdoor Adventures

Chapter 4: Cultural Experiences

Chapter 5: Culinary Delights

Seafood Specialties
Local Markets
Traditional Cape Breton Cuisine
Popular Dining Spots

Chapter 6: Accommodations

Hotels and Resorts
Camping Options

Chapter 7: Practical Information

Currency and Payment
Weather and What to Pack
Safety Tips
Useful Phrases

Chapter 8: Local Events and Festivals

Annual Events Calendar
Participating in Festivals
Community Celebrations

Chapter 9: Additional Tips

Sustainable Travel Practices
Photography Tips
Connecting with Locals

Appendix

Emergency Contacts

Introduction

Embarking on a journey to Cape Breton Island is an exciting venture into the heart of nature's beauty and cultural richness. Nestled on the northeastern tip of Nova Scotia, Canada, Cape Breton is a captivating island that boasts a tapestry of landscapes, from rugged coastlines to lush forests. As you set foot on this enchanting destination, you'll be greeted by the soothing sounds of the Atlantic Ocean, the welcoming warmth of its communities, and the vibrant traditions that have shaped the island's character.

Whether you're drawn to the iconic Cabot Trail, winding through majestic highlands, or yearning for a glimpse of the iconic Peggy's Cove lighthouse, Cape Breton promises a feast for the senses. The island's Gaelic heritage is woven into its very fabric, adding a unique flavor to its music, dance, and festivals. Be prepared to be enchanted by the melodic strains of Celtic tunes that fill the air during ceilidhs, creating an atmosphere that resonates with the island's deep-rooted cultural heritage.

Cape Breton's charm extends beyond its landscapes and traditions to the warmth of its people. From the lively conversations at local pubs to the artisanal crafts found in quaint villages, every corner of the island tells a story. As you traverse its scenic roads and explore hidden gems, you'll find yourself immersed in a world where time seems to slow down, allowing you to savor each moment and appreciate the simple pleasures of life.

So, fasten your seatbelt for a journey filled with breathtaking vistas, cultural discoveries, and the genuine hospitality of Cape Breton's residents. This island promises not just a travel experience but a soulful adventure, inviting you to embrace its beauty, connect with its heritage, and create memories that will linger long after your departure. Welcome to Cape Breton – where nature's wonders and the warmth of community converge to offer an unforgettable escape.

Money/Budget planning

Creating a budget for your stay in Cape Breton Island involves considering various factors. Let's break it down:

Accommodation:
Research and find accommodation options that fit your preferences and budget.
Consider factors like location, amenities, and type of lodging (hotel, Airbnb, etc.).

Transportation:
Estimate costs for getting to Cape Breton Island and transportation within the area.
Include expenses for flights, car rental, or any other means of transport.

Food:
Plan a daily food budget based on your dining preferences.
Consider eating out at restaurants, trying local cuisine, and budgeting for groceries if you plan to cook.

Activities:
Identify activities and attractions you want to experience.
Research entrance fees, tour costs, or any other activity-related expenses.

Miscellaneous:
Set aside funds for unexpected expenses, souvenirs, and other miscellaneous costs.

Duration of Stay:
Determine the number of days you'll be staying to calculate daily expenses.
Now, let's create a sample budget for a

week-long stay:
Accommodation: $800
Transportation: $500 (including flights and car rental)
Food: $300 (assuming $50/day)
Activities: $200
Miscellaneous: $100
Total Budget: $1900

Adjust these estimates based on your specific preferences, lifestyle, and the duration of your stay. It's always wise to have a bit of flexibility in your budget for unexpected expenses.

Welcome to Cape Breton Island

Welcome to Cape Breton Island, a place of breathtaking beauty and warm hospitality! As you embark on your journey to this enchanting island, prepare to be captivated by its stunning landscapes, rich culture, and friendly locals.

Upon arriving, you'll be greeted by the sight of rolling hills, lush forests, and the sparkling waters of the Gulf of St. Lawrence and the Atlantic Ocean. The air is crisp, carrying the scent of the sea, and you'll feel an immediate sense of tranquility as you take in the natural wonders that surround you.

Start your adventure by exploring the famous Cabot Trail, a scenic drive that winds through the Cape Breton Highlands National Park. Marvel at the rugged cliffs, pristine beaches, and panoramic views that make this journey unforgettable. Take your time, stop at lookout points, and breathe in the fresh ocean air.

Immerse yourself in the island's rich Celtic heritage by visiting the Gaelic College in St. Ann's. Here, you can experience traditional music, dance, and crafts that showcase the vibrant cultural tapestry of Cape Breton. Don't miss the opportunity to attend a ceilidh (pronounced kay-lee), a lively gathering filled with music, dance, and community spirit.

Savor the flavors of Cape Breton by indulging in local cuisine. From fresh seafood caught off the shores to hearty dishes that reflect the island's maritime roots, your taste buds are in for a treat. Be sure to try a traditional lobster boil or enjoy a meal at one of the charming seaside restaurants.

As you venture into the charming villages and towns, you'll encounter friendly faces eager to share their stories and make you feel at home. Whether you're exploring the historic streets of Sydney, visiting the iconic lighthouse at Louisbourg, or strolling through the picturesque town of Baddeck, the warmth of the community will leave a lasting impression.

Cape Breton Island welcomes you with open arms, inviting you to immerse yourself in its natural wonders and cultural treasures. Whether you're seeking adventure, relaxation, or a bit of both, this island paradise offers an unforgettable experience that will stay with you long after you've said your farewells. Enjoy your time exploring the magic of Cape Breton!

About this Travel Guide

This travel guide to Cape Breton Island offers a wealth of benefits for anyone planning a visit. Firstly, it provides detailed insights into the island's rich cultural heritage, allowing you to appreciate the local traditions and history. You'll discover the vibrant Gaelic influence, the significance of the Cabot Trail, and the unique blend of Acadian and Mi'kmaq cultures.

Moreover, the guide delves into the breathtaking natural beauty of Cape Breton, describing scenic landscapes, picturesque coastlines, and lush forests. It outlines various outdoor activities such as hiking, whale watching, and exploring the renowned Cabot Links golf course, ensuring you make the most of your time in this stunning setting.

For food enthusiasts, the guide highlights local culinary delights, introducing you to traditional seafood dishes and regional specialties. It provides recommendations for charming restaurants and farmers' markets, allowing you to savor the authentic flavors of Cape Breton.

Additionally, practical information on accommodations, transportation, and local events is included, ensuring a smooth and enjoyable travel experience. From cozy bed-and-breakfasts to modern hotels, the guide helps you find suitable places to stay, catering to different preferences and budgets.

The guide's user-friendly maps and itineraries simplify the planning process, ensuring you don't miss any must-see attractions or hidden gems. Whether you're a history buff, nature lover, or simply seeking a relaxing getaway, the guide tailors its recommendations to diverse interests, making it a valuable resource for every type of traveler.

In essence, this comprehensive travel guide to Cape Breton Island serves as a gateway to an enriching and memorable experience. It goes beyond the basics, immersing you in the island's culture, nature, and local charm, ensuring that your visit is not just a trip but a journey filled with discovery and enjoyment.

How to Use This guide

Using this travel guide can be a great way to make the most of your trip and get the most out of your destination. Here are some tips on how to use a travel guide effectively:
- Read the guidebook cover to cover before your trip to get an overview of the destination and make note of any must-see attractions.
- Bring the guidebook with you during your trip to use as a reference.
- Use the guidebook to find out about local transportation, restaurants, and other practical information.
- Plan your itinerary based on the guidebook's recommendations, but also leave time to explore on your own.

Another important part of using this travel guide effectively is to use it as a resource for finding hidden gems and off-the-beaten-path attractions. The guidebook will likely have information on popular tourist attractions, but it can also be a great resource for finding lesser-known places that are worth visiting. This can help you avoid the crowds and experience the destination like a

local. Additionally, the guidebook can provide valuable information on how to be respectful of local customs and culture.
- Finally, remember that the guidebook is just a starting point for your trip. Allow yourself to be spontaneous and to explore the destination in your own

Chapter 1: Getting Started

Planning Your Trip

Transportation:
Fly into Sydney's J.A. Douglas McCurdy Airport or drive from mainland Nova Scotia.
Car rentals are recommended for exploring the island's scenic routes and hidden gems.

Accommodations:
Choose accommodations based on your preferences, ranging from cozy bed and breakfasts to luxury resorts.
Consider staying in Baddeck for its central location and proximity to the Cabot Trail.

Must-See Attractions:
Cabot Trail: A scenic drive along the island's coastline, offering panoramic views, hiking trails, and wildlife encounters.

Fortress of Louisbourg: Step back in time at this reconstructed 18th-century fortress, where costumed interpreters bring history to life.

Celtic Colours International Festival: If visiting in October, immerse yourself in Cape Breton's rich musical heritage at this renowned festival.

Outdoor Activities:
Hiking enthusiasts can explore trails like the Skyline Trail or the Franey Mountain Trail for stunning vistas.
Whale watching tours depart from various points along the coast, providing opportunities to spot marine life.

Local Cuisine:
Indulge in local delicacies like seafood chowder, lobster, and the famous Cape Breton meat pie.
Visit farmers' markets to sample fresh produce and handmade crafts.

Cultural Immersion:
Attend a ceilidh (pronounced kay-lee), a traditional Gaelic social gathering featuring music, dance, and storytelling.
Engage with local artisans and learn about traditional crafts like rug hooking and pottery.

Weather Preparedness:
Pack layers, as weather conditions can change quickly.
Check the forecast and be prepared for rain, especially during the fall season.

Respect the Environment:
Follow Leave No Trace principles to preserve the natural beauty of the island.
Observe wildlife from a distance and stay on designated trails.

Connect with Locals:
Embrace the island's warm hospitality by striking up conversations with locals who can offer insider tips and recommendations.
By incorporating these elements into your travel plan, you'll create a memorable and enriching experience on Cape Breton island

Transportation Options

Car Rentals:
Convenience: Renting a car is the most convenient way to explore Cape Breton. Several rental agencies operate on the island, providing a hassle-free way to have your own wheels.

Scenic Drives: With well-maintained roads and scenic routes like the Cabot Trail, having a car allows you to set your own pace and take in the mesmerizing views.

Public Transportation:
Bus Services: Cape Breton has a limited but reliable bus service. Check the schedule for routes connecting major towns, making it a cost-effective option for budget-conscious travelers.

Taxis: Taxis are available in towns, offering a flexible way to move around. While more expensive than buses, they provide door-to-door service.

Bicycle Rentals:
Active Exploration: For the more adventurous traveler, renting a bicycle can be a fantastic way to experience the island. Many areas offer bike rentals, letting you explore at a slower pace while enjoying the fresh air.

Shuttle Services:
Guided Tours: Some shuttle services provide guided tours, making it an excellent option for those who prefer a more curated experience. This is a stress-free way to absorb the local culture and history.

Walking:
Town Exploration: Many towns and villages on Cape Breton are pedestrian-friendly, making walking a pleasant way to explore local shops, cafes, and attractions. Take a leisurely stroll and soak in the relaxed atmosphere.

Ferry Services:
Island Hopping: Cape Breton is connected to the mainland by causeways, but ferry services also operate in some areas. Check schedules for a unique and scenic journey between islands.

Ridesharing:
Community Connection: In some areas, ridesharing services may be available, providing an informal and often friendly way to get around. Keep an eye out for local options.
Remember, the transportation choice depends on your preferences and the areas you plan to explore. Whether you opt for the freedom of a rental car, the simplicity of public transportation, or the charm of a guided tour, Cape Breton Island offers a variety of options to suit every traveler's needs.

Getting to Cape Breton

Choose Your Starting Point:
Depending on where you are coming from, you might want to fly into Halifax, Nova Scotia, or Sydney, Cape Breton directly.

Flights to Halifax or Sydney:
If you choose to fly, book a flight to either Halifax Stanfield International Airport (YHZ) or J.A. Douglas McCurdy Sydney Airport (YQY). Halifax is a major airport with more flight options.

Connecting to Cape Breton:
From Halifax, you can either rent a car and drive to Cape Breton (approximately a 4-hour scenic drive) or take a shuttle service. Alternatively, you can book a connecting flight to Sydney if available.

Rental Cars and Transportation:
Once you arrive in Sydney or Halifax, consider renting a car for flexibility in exploring Cape Breton. If you prefer not to drive, there are also bus services and guided tours available.

Scenic Drive:
If you decide to drive, the Cabot Trail is a must. It's a picturesque route that takes you around the island, offering stunning coastal views and mountainous landscapes.

Ferry Option:
Another unique option is taking the ferry from Nova Scotia's mainland to Cape Breton. The ferry operates between North Sydney and Marine Atlantic Ferry Terminal in North Sydney.

Chapter 2: Exploring Regions

Cabot Trail

Cabot Trail

Starting your exploration in Baddeck, a quaint village on the shores of Bras d'Or Lake, you'll soon find yourself surrounded by lush greenery and coastal beauty. The Cabot Trail winds its way through Cape Breton Highlands National Park, where rugged cliffs meet the Atlantic Ocean, creating a dramatic and awe-inspiring backdrop.

Driving along the trail, you'll encounter several lookout points, such as the iconic Skyline Trail, providing panoramic views of the Gulf of St. Lawrence. Keep your eyes peeled for wildlife, as moose and bald eagles are often spotted in this natural haven.

As you continue, the trail weaves through Acadian fishing villages like Chéticamp, offering a glimpse into the island's rich cultural tapestry. Sample local cuisine, including freshly caught seafood, in one of the charming restaurants that dot the trail.

The journey doesn't just showcase natural beauty; it also immerses you in Cape Breton's vibrant Celtic heritage. Stop at the Glenora Distillery, where you can savor world-class single malt whisky and enjoy the warm hospitality of the locals.

Venture further to Ingonish, where the coastline transforms into sandy beaches and pristine coves. Take a detour to Middle Head Trail for a refreshing hike along the rugged coastline.

As you reach the northern part of the island, the trail descends to the charming town of Bay St. Lawrence, known for its rugged cliffs and whale-watching opportunities. The winding roads and coastal vistas make every turn a discovery, creating an unforgettable experience.

In summary, the Cabot Trail is a must-visit for nature lovers, adventure seekers, and those who appreciate the rich tapestry of culture and history. Each curve of the road unveils a new facet of Cape Breton's beauty, leaving you with cherished memories of this enchanting journey.

Hiking Trails

For those seeking a coastal experience, the Cabot Trail Coastal Loop is an excellent choice. This trail meanders along the Atlantic shoreline, offering glimpses of dramatic cliffs and the vast ocean. The easy-to-moderate difficulty level makes it accessible for hikers of various skill levels.

The Franey Trail

Inland, the Franey Trail beckons adventurers with a mix of forested paths and open plateaus. The climb is moderately strenuous, but the summit unveils sweeping views of the Clyburn Valley and the Gulf of St. Lawrence. It's a great trail for those looking to immerse themselves in the island's wilderness.

The Jack Pine Trail

The Jack Pine Trail, near Ingonish, is another gem. This short and easy hike takes you through an enchanting forest, leading to a serene beach. It's an ideal spot for a leisurely stroll and a picnic, surrounded by the tranquility of nature.

If you're up for a more challenging trek, the Pollett's Cove Trail is a backcountry adventure. This longer hike takes you to a remote cove where you can experience the untamed beauty of Cape Breton's wilderness. Be prepared for a full day of hiking and breathtaking scenery.

Remember to check trail conditions and weather forecasts before embarking on your journey. Pack essentials like water, snacks, and appropriate clothing, and always follow Leave No Trace principles to preserve the natural beauty of Cape Breton Island. Happy hiking!

Sydney and Surroundings

Sydney and its surroundings offer a delightful blend of natural beauty and cultural richness for your journey to Cape Breton Island. Sydney, situated on the eastern side of the island, is a charming waterfront city known for its warm hospitality.

As you explore Sydney, take a stroll along the picturesque waterfront boardwalk. Admire the view of the harbor and watch fishing boats gently bobbing in the water. You'll find quaint shops and cafes, providing a perfect opportunity to sample local cuisine and perhaps indulge in freshly caught seafood.

Venture into the heart of Sydney to discover the Cape Breton Centre for Heritage and Science. This cultural gem showcases the island's history through engaging exhibits, offering insights into the vibrant traditions of the community. Don't miss the chance to explore the historic district, where well-preserved buildings reflect the city's maritime past.

Heading out from Sydney towards Cape Breton, the scenic Cabot Trail awaits. This iconic route takes you through breathtaking landscapes, with lush forests, rugged coastlines, and panoramic views. Keep your camera ready as you wind your way through the Cape Breton Highlands National Park, where the vibrant colors of the scenery are truly awe-inspiring.

Make a stop at the Cape Breton Miners' Museum in Glace Bay to delve into the island's coal mining history. The museum offers a fascinating journey into the lives of coal miners, providing a unique perspective on the region's industrial heritage.

Continue your adventure to Baddeck, a charming village on the shores of the Bras d'Or Lake. Visit the Alexander Graham Bell National Historic Site, dedicated to the inventor of the telephone. The museum houses intriguing artifacts and exhibits, shedding light on Bell's life and accomplishments.

In Ingonish, embrace the tranquility of Ingonish Beach and the stunning vistas of Middle Head Peninsula. The Cape Smokey Provincial Park offers an opportunity for a scenic hike, rewarding you with panoramic views of the Gulf of St. Lawrence.

As you conclude your journey in Cape Breton, take a moment to appreciate the island's unique blend of culture, history, and natural wonders. Whether you're exploring the vibrant city of Sydney or immersing yourself in the beauty of the Cabot Trail, your adventure promises to be a memorable exploration of Cape Breton's diverse offerings.

Historic Sites

As you explore this picturesque island, be sure to visit these captivating destinations:

Fortress of Louisbourg

Fortress of Louisbourg: Step back in time to the 18th century at the Fortress of Louisbourg, a meticulously reconstructed French fortress. Wander through the cobbled streets, interact with costumed interpreters, and experience life as it was during the peak of the French colonial era.

Alexander Graham Bell National Historic Site

Alexander Graham Bell National Historic Site: Discover the legacy of the inventor of the telephone at the Alexander Graham Bell National Historic Site in Baddeck. Explore exhibits showcasing Bell's inventions, his contributions to aviation, and his deep connection to Cape Breton.

Cabot Trail

Cabot Trail: While primarily known for its breathtaking scenery, the Cabot Trail also boasts historical significance. The route takes you through areas settled by Scottish and Acadian communities, offering glimpses of traditional architecture and remnants of early settlements.

St. Patrick's Church Museum

St. Patrick's Church Museum: Located in Sydney, St. Patrick's Church Museum provides insight into Cape Breton's Irish heritage. The museum, housed in a stunning historic church, displays artifacts and exhibits related to the Irish immigration and the development of the local community.

Highland Village Museum

Highland Village Museum: Immerse yourself in the Scottish Gaelic culture at the Highland Village Museum in Iona. This living history museum showcases period buildings and interpreters portraying the daily lives of early Scottish settlers, providing a vivid representation of Cape Breton's cultural tapestry.

Old sydney Society Museums

Old Sydney Society Museums: Explore the Old Sydney Society Museums, including the Cossit House and the Jost House, which offer a glimpse into daily life during different periods of Cape Breton's history. These well-preserved homes showcase the island's architectural evolution.

L'Ardoise Chapel: Visit the charming L'Ardoise Chapel, a historic church that reflects the area's Acadian heritage. Admire its simple yet elegant design, and learn about the role it played in the community's religious and cultural life.

Louisbourg Lighthouse Coastal Trail

Louisbourg Lighthouse Coastal Trail: While enjoying the stunning coastal views along this trail, you'll also encounter remnants of early settlements, including the remains of the Louisbourg Lighthouse. This serene path offers both natural beauty and a connection to Cape Breton's maritime history.

As you embark on your journey through Cape Breton Island, these historic sites will not only transport you through time but also provide a deeper understanding of the island's cultural mosaic. Enjoy your travels!

Waterfront Activities

Begin your day with a serene stroll along the shoreline, feeling the gentle breeze and taking in the breathtaking views of the Atlantic Ocean.

For those seeking a more active experience, kayaking is a popular choice. Paddle along the coastline, exploring hidden coves and enjoying the company of seabirds. Many local outfitters offer kayak rentals and guided tours, ensuring a safe and enjoyable experience for all skill levels.

Fishing enthusiasts can try their luck at the island's abundant fishing spots. Whether you're a novice or an experienced angler, you can cast your line into the clear waters and try to reel in a variety of fish species. Local charters are available for those who prefer a guided fishing excursion.

If you prefer a more laid-back activity, pack a picnic and unwind on one of the island's sandy beaches. Listen to the soothing sound of waves while basking in the warmth of the sun. Some beaches even have designated fire pits, allowing you to end your day with a cozy beachfront bonfire under the starry Cape Breton sky.

For a taste of local culture, attend a beachside music festival or join a community gathering by the water. Cape Breton is known for its vibrant folk music scene, and you might find impromptu performances along the waterfront, creating an atmosphere of joy and celebration.

To explore the marine life in the region, consider taking a boat tour. Knowledgeable guides will share insights about the coastal ecosystem, and you might be lucky enough to spot seals, whales, and other wildlife in their natural habitat.

As the day winds down, treat yourself to a seafood feast at one of the waterfront restaurants. Indulge in freshly caught lobster or enjoy a bowl of clam chowder while relishing the stunning sunset over the water.

In conclusion, Cape Breton Island's waterfront activities cater to a diverse range of interests, providing a memorable experience for every traveler. Whether you seek adventure, relaxation, or a blend of both, the island's coastal charm will undoubtedly leave a lasting impression on your travel memories.

Dining and Entertainment

you'll find a variety of options that cater to different tastes.

Dining:
Seafood Extravaganza: Being surrounded by the Atlantic Ocean, Cape Breton is renowned for its fresh seafood. Indulge in delectable lobster, succulent scallops, and perfectly cooked fish at waterfront restaurants like The Lobster Pound.

Traditional Fare: Immerse yourself in local flavors with traditional Cape Breton dishes. Try the iconic meat pie, known as "tourtière," or sample a hearty bowl of seafood chowder, which showcases the region's culinary heritage.

Cozy Cafés: For a more relaxed atmosphere, explore charming cafés scattered across the island. Sip on locally roasted coffee while enjoying homemade pastries and desserts at spots like The Cape Beanery.

Entertainment:

Ceilidh Music: Cape Breton is famous for its lively Celtic music scene. Attend a ceilidh, a traditional Gaelic gathering featuring spirited music and dance. Venues like the Red Shoe Pub in Mabou are perfect for an authentic experience.

Festivals and Events: Plan your visit around one of Cape Breton's many festivals. The Celtic Colours International Festival, held in October, is a highlight, showcasing a vibrant mix of music, dance, and community spirit.

Cultural Shows: Immerse yourself in the island's rich cultural heritage by attending performances that showcase local traditions. Look for events featuring step dancing, fiddling, and storytelling.

Artisan Markets: Explore artisan markets where local craftsmen display their talents. From handmade jewelry to traditional crafts, these markets offer a unique shopping experience.

Hiking and Dining: Combine outdoor adventure with dining by exploring the island's scenic trails. After a day of hiking, unwind at a cozy inn or restaurant, savoring a well-deserved meal with breathtaking views.

Whether you're seeking a taste of local cuisine or an evening filled with music and dance, Cape Breton Island ensures a delightful journey blending dining and entertainment.

Chapter 3: Outdoor Adventures

Whale watching

The best time for whale watching in Cape Breton is typically from May to October, when various species, including humpback whales, minke whales, and even the elusive blue whales, migrate through the area. The tours are led by knowledgeable guides who share interesting facts about the marine life and the region's rich maritime history.

Once aboard the comfortable boat, you'll cruise through the Atlantic waters, where the cool sea breeze and the sound of waves create a soothing atmosphere. Keep your eyes peeled, and you might spot the distinctive spouts of whales breaking the surface. Cameras ready, as these moments are not only mesmerizing but also perfect for capturing memories of your adventure.

The excitement peaks when a massive whale breaches, leaping gracefully out of the water, creating a spectacle that leaves everyone on board in awe. The guides provide engaging commentary, helping you identify different species and explaining their behaviors. Children and adults alike are captivated by the sheer size and grace of these marine giants.

Cape Breton's coastline itself is a sight to behold, with rugged cliffs and picturesque landscapes that serve as a backdrop to your whale watching expedition. The tours often include additional sightings of seabirds, seals, and other marine life, enhancing the overall experience.

After a memorable day at sea, you may find yourself reflecting on the unique connection you've forged with the ocean and its incredible inhabitants. Whether you're a nature enthusiast or simply seeking a magical encounter with wildlife, whale watching in Cape Breton promises an unforgettable journey into the heart of the Atlantic's wonders.

Bird Watching

Here's a detailed guide to enhance your bird-watching adventure:

Scenic Locations:
Begin your bird-watching expedition at iconic spots like the Cape Breton Highlands National Park, where boreal forests and coastal cliffs create an ideal habitat. Explore the Cabot Trail, winding through picturesque landscapes that showcase both inland and marine bird species.

Seasonal Diversity:
The best time to visit is during spring and fall migrations when birds are on the move. Spring welcomes warblers and waterfowl, while fall brings raptors and shorebirds. The island's seasonal changes promise a dynamic array of feathered residents and visitors.

Essential Gear:
Arm yourself with basic bird-watching equipment, including binoculars, a field guide, and a notebook to document your sightings. Wear muted colors to blend into the surroundings, increasing your chances of observing birds in their natural habitat.

Notable Species:
Cape Breton boasts a rich avian population, including the iconic Atlantic Puffin, Bald Eagle, and the elusive Bicknell's Thrush. Keep an eye out for seabirds along the coast and songbirds nestled in the lush woodlands.

Trail Exploration:
Traverse the island's well-maintained trails, such as the Skyline Trail, where you may encounter the majestic Northern Gannet soaring above or spot a Peregrine Falcon perched on a rocky outcrop. The Franey Trail is another gem, offering a chance to witness warblers in the spring.

Coastal Birding:
The coastal regions of Cape Breton provide a unique opportunity to observe seabirds. Look for Great Cormorants, Common Eiders, and Black Guillemots as they navigate the Atlantic shores.

Community Engagement:
Engage with local bird-watching communities or guided tours to gain insights from experienced enthusiasts. They can share valuable tips and may point out rare species you might miss on your own.

Conservation Awareness:
While enjoying the avian wonders, remember to respect the environment. Keep a safe distance from nesting sites, avoid disturbing the birds, and adhere to conservation guidelines to preserve Cape Breton's natural beauty for future generations.

Weather Considerations:
Be mindful of Cape Breton's ever-changing weather. Dress in layers, pack rain gear, and check the weather forecast to ensure a comfortable and enjoyable bird-watching experience.

Memorable Moments:
Capture the essence of your bird-watching journey by documenting your sightings and taking photographs. Reflect on the serene moments spent in nature and the diverse avian life that makes Cape Breton Island a bird-watching paradise.

Cape Breton Island invites you to unravel the mysteries of its avian residents amid breathtaking landscapes, promising an enriching and memorable bird-watching escapade.

Kayaking and Canoeing

Begin your exploration at the iconic Cabot Trail, where the Atlantic Ocean meets the island's rugged shores. Launch your kayak or canoe into the calm waters, and you'll find yourself immersed in the tranquility of the Gulf of St. Lawrence. The vibrant hues of the sky paint a stunning backdrop as you navigate through the crystal-clear waters.

Make your way towards the Bras d'Or Lake, a vast inland sea nestled within the island. Glide through the mirror-like surface, surrounded by rolling hills and dense forests. Keep an eye out for the diverse wildlife that calls this region home – from majestic eagles soaring overhead to playful seals bobbing in the water.

As you paddle, take breaks along the hidden coves and secluded beaches that dot the coastline. These idyllic spots offer a perfect opportunity to rest, enjoy a picnic, and absorb the natural beauty that Cape Breton Island generously offers. The sandy shores invite you to stretch your legs, while the melodious sounds of nature provide a soundtrack to your peaceful interlude.

Venture into the vibrant fishing villages along the coast, where friendly locals share tales of maritime traditions. The colorful boats lining the harbors and the aroma of freshly caught seafood create a sensory experience that adds to the richness of your journey.

As the day winds down, find a suitable campsite along the shoreline. Setting up your tent under a star-studded sky, you'll be captivated by the tranquility of the island. The sound of lapping waves and distant calls of nocturnal wildlife lull you into a peaceful slumber, ready to awaken to another day of exploration.

Cape Breton Island's kayaking and canoeing adventure is not just a physical journey; it's a soul-enriching experience that connects you with the raw beauty of nature. With each paddle stroke, you'll create memories that linger long after the journey ends – a testament to the simplicity and wonder of this captivating island escape.

Beaches and Coastal Exploration

Ingonish Beach:

Ingonish Beach

Start your coastal adventure at Ingonish Beach, a picturesque sandy stretch with crystal-clear waters. You can relax on the beach, take a refreshing swim, or explore the nearby hiking trails offering panoramic views of the ocean and surrounding hills.

Cabot Trail:

Cabot Trail

Embark on the famous Cabot Trail, winding along the island's rugged cliffs and offering breathtaking vistas. The coastal drive takes you through quaint fishing villages, where you can witness the charm of local maritime life.

White Point Beach:

White Point Beach

White Point Beach invites you to experience the tranquility of a pristine sandy shore. Walk along the coastline, collecting seashells and enjoying the sound of the waves crashing against the shore. The view of the open sea is mesmerizing.

Louisbourg Lighthouse Coastal Trail:

Louisbourg Lighthouse Coastal Trail

For a historical and scenic blend, explore the Louisbourg Lighthouse Coastal Trail. The trail offers a glimpse into the island's maritime history while providing stunning views of the rugged coastline and the vastness of the Atlantic Ocean.

Mabou Coastal Loop:

Mabou Coastal Loop

If you're up for a more immersive experience, take the Mabou Coastal Loop. This trail not only offers coastal views but also takes you through lush landscapes and charming villages, allowing you to connect with the local culture.

Bay St. Lawrence:

Bay St. Lawrence

Venture to Bay St. Lawrence, where the coastal scenery reaches new heights. The cliffs overlook the Gulf of St. Lawrence, and the dramatic landscape is a photographer's dream. Keep an eye out for marine life, as this area is known for whale watching.

Black Brook Beach:

Black Brook Beach

Relax at Black Brook Beach, a secluded spot with golden sands and clear waters. It's an ideal place to unwind, have a picnic, and enjoy the serene beauty of Cape Breton's coastline away from the crowds.

Seal Island Bridge:

Seal Island Bridge

Cross the Seal Island Bridge and take a moment to admire the panoramic views of the Bras d'Or Lake. The bridge connects the island, providing a unique perspective of the waterway's vastness.

Chapter 4: Cultural Experiences

Gaelic Heritage

The Gaelic culture has left an indelible mark on the island, shaping its traditions, music, dance, and language.

Gaelic Language:
One of the most significant aspects of Cape Breton's Gaelic heritage is the preservation of the Gaelic language. Although it has faced challenges over the years, there are still communities where Gaelic is spoken and taught. You might encounter Gaelic signage, and locals may greet you with traditional Gaelic phrases, adding a unique linguistic flavor to your experience.

Music and Dance:
Cape Breton is renowned for its vibrant Celtic music and dance scene. The island's traditional fiddle music, often accompanied by the bagpipes, reflects its Gaelic roots. Attend a ceilidh (pronounced kay-lee), a lively social gathering featuring traditional music and dance, to immerse yourself in the spirited rhythms of the Gaelic culture.

Cultural Events:
Throughout the year, Cape Breton hosts various cultural events celebrating its Gaelic heritage. Festivals, workshops, and gatherings provide opportunities to witness and participate in traditional activities, fostering a deeper understanding of the island's rich cultural tapestry.

Historical Sites:
Explore historical sites such as the Highland Village Museum, a living history museum that recreates a 19th-century Gaelic settlement. This immersive experience allows you to step back in time and appreciate the daily lives, customs, and traditions of the early Gaelic settlers.

Gaelic Heritage Trails:
Embark on the Gaelic Heritage Trails that wind through the island, connecting various cultural and historical sites. These trails offer a scenic journey through landscapes that have shaped the Gaelic heritage of Cape Breton.

Community Involvement:
Engage with the local Gaelic community, attending gatherings and perhaps participating in Gaelic language workshops or traditional crafts. This direct interaction will provide you with insights into the resilience and vibrancy of Cape Breton's Gaelic heritage.

Art and Craftsmanship:
Discover local artisans who continue traditional Gaelic craftsmanship, producing items such as woolen goods, pottery, and intricate Celtic designs. These creations often blend old-world techniques with contemporary influences, showcasing the enduring creativity of the Gaelic heritage.

By embracing the Gaelic heritage of Cape Breton Island, you'll not only witness a unique cultural tapestry but also become part of a living legacy that continues to thrive in this picturesque Canadian destination.

Celtic Music and Festivals

Celtic Music in Cape Breton:
Cape Breton's Celtic music is deeply rooted in Scottish and Irish traditions, brought by early settlers. Fiddles play a central role, creating lively melodies that capture the spirit of the island. Traditional tunes, passed down through generations, are skillfully performed by talented musicians, often in lively sessions at local pubs or community gatherings.

Instruments:
The fiddle takes the lead in many Celtic compositions, accompanied by instruments like the guitar, accordion, and piano. Bagpipes also make a significant impact, adding a haunting and majestic quality to the music. The combination of these instruments creates a unique sound that resonates with the island's Celtic heritage.

Festivals:
Cape Breton hosts several festivals that celebrate its Celtic musical heritage. One notable event is the Celtic Colours International Festival, held annually in October. This festival showcases local and international talent, featuring concerts, workshops, and community events. The vivid autumn landscape provides a breathtaking backdrop for the festivities, attracting music enthusiasts from around the world.

Celtic Colours International Festival:
During the Celtic Colours Festival, Cape Breton comes alive with the sounds of fiddles, bagpipes, and the energetic footwork of step dancers. Concerts are held in various venues across the island, from historic churches to community halls, creating an intimate and immersive experience. The festival not only highlights traditional Celtic music but also explores contemporary expressions of this rich musical heritage.

Community Engagement:
Cape Breton's Celtic music is not just a performance; it's a communal experience. Many festivals and events encourage audience participation, whether through dancing, singing along, or joining in on impromptu jam sessions. This sense of community engagement adds a special charm to the music scene, fostering a connection between performers and attendees.

Local Influences:
Beyond the festivals, visitors can explore the local music scene in pubs and venues throughout Cape Breton. Musicians often draw inspiration from the island's landscapes, history, and the warmth of its communities, infusing their performances with a genuine and heartfelt quality.

In conclusion, a journey to Cape Breton Island offers a captivating immersion into the world of Celtic music. From the soul-stirring melodies to the lively festivals, visitors can experience the island's rich cultural heritage through its vibrant musical traditions.

Museums and Art Galleries

Cape Breton Centre for Craft and Design:
Located in Sydney, this center celebrates the rich tradition of craftsmanship in Cape Breton. Visitors can explore various exhibits showcasing local artisans' work, attend workshops, and even purchase unique handmade crafts as souvenirs.

Art Gallery of Nova Scotia – Sydney:
As an extension of the provincial gallery, the Sydney branch features rotating exhibitions of both historical and contemporary Nova Scotian art. It's a great place to get a sense of the region's artistic evolution.

Cossit House Museum:
Situated in Sydney, this museum offers a glimpse into the daily life of early 19th-century Cape Breton. The well-preserved house displays period furniture, textiles, and artifacts, providing a fascinating look into the island's history.

Cape Breton Miners' Museum:
In Glace Bay, this museum pays homage to the region's coal mining heritage. It includes exhibits on the lives of miners, the tools they used, and the challenges they faced. The highlight is an underground tour, offering a unique experience of a miner's working conditions.

Highland Village Museum:
Located in Iona, this living history museum showcases Nova Scotian Gaelic culture. Visitors can explore historic buildings, interact with costumed interpreters, and learn about the traditions and daily life of the Gaelic settlers.

St. Patrick's Museum:
Found in North Sydney, this museum focuses on the Irish heritage of Cape Breton. Exhibits cover topics such as immigration, cultural traditions, and the contributions of the Irish community to the development of the island.

Lyceum - Cape Breton University Art Gallery:
Situated at Cape Breton University, this gallery hosts a variety of contemporary art exhibitions. It's a dynamic space that often features works by local and regional artists, providing a platform for emerging talent.

Remember to check opening hours and any COVID-19 related guidelines before visiting these attractions. Enjoy your trip to Cape
Breton Island!

Chapter 5: Culinary Delights

Seafood Specialties

prepare to tantalize your taste buds with an array of fresh and savory delights.

1. Lobster:
Indulge in the succulent flavor of Cape Breton's renowned lobster. Served steamed or grilled, this local delicacy is best enjoyed with melted butter, allowing the sweet, tender meat to shine. Lobster festivals are common during the season, providing a delightful opportunity to savor this maritime treasure.

2. Digby Scallops:
Savor the buttery goodness of Digby scallops, known for their exceptional quality and taste. Often pan-seared to perfection, these plump mollusks offer a delicate and delectable seafood experience. Pair them with locally sourced vegetables for a wholesome feast.

3. Snow Crab:
Cape Breton is also celebrated for its bountiful snow crab harvest. Experience the sweet and flaky meat of these crustaceans, typically served in clusters and accompanied by zesty dipping sauces. Enjoying a crab boil is a communal and flavorful way to relish this maritime delight.

4. Mussels:
Immerse yourself in the rich flavors of Cape Breton mussels. Often prepared in a delectable white wine and garlic broth, these shellfish provide a taste of the region's coastal charm. Dive into a bowl of steaming mussels and savor the freshness of the Atlantic Ocean.

5. Fisherman's Brewis:
For a taste of traditional Cape Breton fare, try Fisherman's Brewis—a hearty dish featuring salted fish, hardtack biscuits, and scrunchions (crispy bits of salted pork). This comfort food reflects the island's seafaring history and provides a unique culinary experience.

6. Seafood Chowder:
Warm your soul with a bowl of Cape Breton's seafood chowder, a creamy and hearty concoction brimming with an assortment of locally sourced seafood, potatoes, and aromatic herbs. It's the perfect dish to savor on a cool Maritime evening.

As you traverse Cape Breton Island, let the sea-to-table experience enchant you. From lobster shacks to fine dining establishments, the region's seafood specialties promise a gastronomic adventure, inviting you to savor the essence of its maritime culture. Bon appétit!

Local Markets

As you meander through the stalls, you'll encounter friendly vendors eager to share stories about their offerings. Sample the assortment of locally grown fruits, vegetables, and artisanal cheeses, each item telling a tale of the island's fertile landscapes.

Don't miss the opportunity to engage with skilled artisans who proudly display their handcrafted wares. From intricately woven textiles to meticulously carved wooden pieces, the market is a treasure trove of Cape Breton craftsmanship.

For a taste of the island's maritime heritage, visit the Sydney Fish Market. Here, the day's catch is showcased in abundance. The briny scent of the ocean mingles with the lively chatter of fishmongers, creating an authentic maritime experience. Choose from a variety of fresh seafood, from succulent lobster to perfectly smoked salmon, and savor the flavors that define Cape Breton's coastal identity.

As you explore the local markets, you'll undoubtedly encounter traditional Cape Breton music and dance. Live performances often grace these bustling spaces, providing a soundtrack to your market adventure. Feel the rhythm of the island as you shop, adding an extra layer of cultural richness to your experience.

In Baddeck, the heart of Cape Breton's scenic beauty, the Baddeck Farmers' Market is a must-visit. Against the backdrop of the Bras d'Or Lake, this market captures the essence of community, offering a diverse array of products that reflect the region's distinct character.

Take your time to appreciate the warm hospitality of the locals, who are more than happy to share recommendations for hidden gems and off-the-beaten-path treasures. Whether you're searching for unique souvenirs, indulging in local delicacies, or simply immersing yourself in the vibrant community atmosphere, Cape Breton's local markets promise an enriching and memorable experience.

Traditional Cape Breton Cuisine

Traditional Cape Breton cuisine reflects the rich maritime heritage of the island, with a focus on fresh and locally sourced ingredients. One culinary gem you shouldn't miss is the iconic Cape Breton lobster. Served in various forms, from succulent lobster rolls to hearty lobster chowder, this delicacy showcases the island's connection to the Atlantic Ocean.

Another staple is the Cape Breton meat pie, a savory dish featuring a flaky crust filled with a hearty blend of minced meat, onions, and spices. It's a comfort food that has stood the test of time, passed down through generations.

For a taste of the sea, try the famous fisherman's brewis. This dish consists of salt fish soaked overnight and then boiled with hard bread, potatoes, and pork fat. It's a hearty and flavorful dish that originated from the island's fishing communities.

In the realm of sweets, don't forget to indulge in a slice of Cape Breton oatcake. These dense and buttery treats are made with oats, flour, and butter, creating a delightful combination of sweetness and crunch. They are often enjoyed with a cup of tea, providing a cozy and comforting experience.

Exploring the island's farmers' markets is a great way to sample a variety of local produce, including wild blueberries, apples, and artisanal cheeses. The freshness of these ingredients adds a vibrant touch to Cape Breton's culinary offerings.

Lastly, immerse yourself in the warmth of Cape Breton hospitality by attending a traditional kitchen party. These gatherings involve lively music, storytelling, and, of course, delicious food. It's a perfect opportunity to experience the community spirit and savor the authentic flavors of Cape Breton.

In conclusion, Cape Breton's cuisine is a celebration of its maritime roots, featuring a diverse array of dishes that showcase the island's natural bounty. From lobster to meat pies and oatcakes, each bite tells a story of tradition and local pride. Enjoy your culinary adventure on this picturesque island!

Popular Dining Spots

The Red Shoe Pub (Mabou):
Located in the heart of Mabou, The Red Shoe Pub is a cozy spot known for its warm atmosphere and live Celtic music. Treat your taste buds to traditional Nova Scotian dishes, including fresh seafood and hearty pub fare.

Governors Pub & Eatery (Sydney):
In Sydney, Governors Pub & Eatery combines a historic setting with a diverse menu. Enjoy waterfront views as you savor seafood chowder, lobster, and other regional specialties. The lively pub also hosts live music events.

Flavor on the Water (Sydney):
Overlooking the Sydney waterfront, Flavor on the Water offers a sophisticated dining experience. The menu features a fusion of local ingredients and international flavors, ensuring a diverse range of options for every palate.

Dancing Moose Café (Ingonish Beach):
If you find yourself near Ingonish Beach, the Dancing Moose Café is a charming stop. Known for its delicious breakfast options and freshly baked goods, it's a favorite among locals and visitors alike.

Chanterelle Country Inn & Cottages

Restaurant (Baddeck):
For a more intimate dining experience, visit the Chanterelle Country Inn & Cottages Restaurant in Baddeck. This fine dining establishment focuses on seasonal and locally sourced ingredients, providing a taste of Cape Breton's culinary delights.

Celtic Music Interpretive Centre (Judique):
Combine music and dining at the Celtic Music Interpretive Centre in Judique. Enjoy traditional Celtic tunes while savoring a meal that showcases the region's flavors. The cultural experience makes this spot unique.

Seagull Restaurant (Louisbourg):
In Louisbourg, the Seagull Restaurant offers a casual dining experience with a focus on seafood. From lobster rolls to fish and chips, you'll find a variety of maritime delights to enjoy in this seaside town.

Highland Bistro (Inverness):
If you're in Inverness, make sure to visit the Highland Bistro. This restaurant combines a relaxed atmosphere with a menu that celebrates local produce. Enjoy a meal with a view of the stunning Cape Breton landscape.
As you embark on your culinary journey through Cape Breton Island, these dining spots promise not only delicious food but also a glimpse into the rich cultural tapestry of this beautiful region.

Chapter 6: Accommodations

Hotels and Resorts

Cape Breton Island is a stunning destination with a variety of hotels and resorts to enhance your travel experience.

Keltic Lodge Resort and Spa:
Nestled on the edge of the world-renowned Cape Breton Highlands National Park, Keltic Lodge offers breathtaking views of the Gulf of St. Lawrence. With cozy rooms and a spa for relaxation, it's a perfect blend of comfort and nature.

Inverary Resort:
Overlooking Baddeck Bay, Inverary Resort combines classic charm with modern amenities. Enjoy waterfront cottages, an indoor pool, and fine dining options. It's an ideal choice for those seeking tranquility.

Silver Dart Lodge:
Situated near the Bras d'Or Lake, Silver Dart Lodge provides a peaceful retreat. The lodge offers comfortable accommodations and is close to the historic village of Baddeck, making it convenient for exploring local attractions.

The Lakes at Ben Eoin Golf Club & Resort:
Golf enthusiasts will appreciate this resort overlooking the Bras d'Or Lakes. Aside from the golf course, there are luxurious accommodations, dining options, and outdoor activities like hiking and kayaking.

Hampton Inn Sydney:
If you prefer staying in the city, Hampton Inn in Sydney offers a central location with easy access to local shops and restaurants. The hotel provides modern amenities, a fitness center, and a complimentary breakfast.

Cabot Links Lodge:
Golfers and nature lovers alike will enjoy Cabot Links Lodge. Overlooking the Gulf of St. Lawrence, it offers world-class golf courses and upscale accommodations. The design reflects the coastal beauty of Cape Breton.

Dundee Resort and Golf Club:
Set on the shores of the Bras d'Or Lakes, Dundee Resort provides a range of activities, from golf to water sports. The resort features comfortable rooms, dining options, and stunning sunset views.

Whether you seek the tranquility of nature or the convenience of city accommodations, Cape Breton Island's hotels and resorts cater to various preferences, ensuring a memorable and comfortable stay during your travels.

Camping Options

Here are some detailed camping choices for your trip:

National Parks:
Cape Breton Highlands National Park: This park boasts several campgrounds, including Broad Cove, Ingonish Beach, and Chéticamp. Each site offers various amenities such as fire pits, picnic tables, and washroom facilities. The landscapes range from coastal cliffs to lush forests, providing diverse camping experiences.

Provincial Parks:
Whycocomagh Provincial Park: Nestled on the shores of Whycocomagh Bay, this park provides a serene camping environment. Facilities include electricity, showers, and access to hiking trails. It's an excellent choice for both RV and tent camping.

Private Campgrounds:
Baddeck Cabot Trail Campground: Situated near the iconic Cabot Trail, this private campground offers a mix of wooded and open sites. With amenities like hot showers, laundry, and a camp store, it provides a comfortable camping experience while being close to attractions like the Alexander Graham Bell National Historic Site.

Backcountry Camping:
Pollett's Cove: For those seeking a more rugged experience, consider backcountry camping at Pollett's Cove. Accessible by a hike or boat, this secluded spot offers a true wilderness experience. Be sure to bring all necessary supplies as amenities are minimal.

Glamping Options:
Cabot Shores Wilderness Resort: If you prefer a touch of luxury in the great outdoors, consider glamping at Cabot Shores. They offer accommodations ranging from yurts to domes, providing a unique blend of comfort and nature.

RV Parks:
North Sydney RV Park: Ideal for those traveling in recreational vehicles, this park offers full-service sites with water, electricity, and sewage hookups. Conveniently located near the ferry terminal, it's a practical choice for travelers arriving or departing via the ferry.
Remember to check availability and make reservations in advance, especially during peak seasons. Whether you prefer the comforts of established campgrounds or the tranquility of backcountry camping, Cape Breton Island has diverse options to suit every camper's preference. Enjoy your outdoor adventure!

Chapter 7: Practical Information

Currency and Payment

Currency and payments play a crucial role when traveling to Cape Breton Island. In this picturesque destination, the primary currency used is the Canadian Dollar (CAD). It's essential to be familiar with the local currency to ensure smooth transactions during your stay.

1. Currency Exchange:
Before embarking on your journey, consider exchanging your home currency for Canadian Dollars. You can do this at banks, currency exchange offices, or even at the airport. Keep in mind that rates may vary, so it's advisable to compare options to get the best deal.

2. Credit and Debit Cards:
Credit and debit cards are widely accepted in Cape Breton, especially in larger establishments like hotels, restaurants, and retail stores. Make sure to inform your bank about your travel plans to avoid any potential issues with card transactions. While cards are convenient, it's wise to carry some cash for places that might not accept cards.

3. ATMs:
ATMs are readily available in urban areas, providing a convenient way to withdraw Canadian Dollars. Keep in mind that some ATMs may charge fees for international transactions, so it's advisable to check with your bank beforehand.

4. Cash Usage:
Despite the prevalence of electronic payments, having some cash on hand is beneficial, particularly in more remote areas or smaller businesses that may not accept cards. You'll find ATMs in major towns, allowing you to replenish your cash supply as needed.

5. Tipping Culture:
Tipping is customary in Canada, and it's expected to leave a gratuity in restaurants, taxis, and for other services. A standard tip is around 15-20% of the total bill. Ensure you have enough cash for tipping situations where card payments may not be as convenient.

6. Mobile Payments:
Mobile payment options, such as Apple Pay or Google Pay, are becoming increasingly popular. Check if these options are accepted in the places you plan to visit, as they offer a convenient and contactless way to make payments.

In summary, a combination of credit/debit cards, cash, and possibly mobile payments will cover your payment needs on Cape Breton Island. It's always wise to have a variety of payment methods to ensure you're prepared for different situations. Enjoy your travels!

Weather and What to Pack

When planning your trip, it's essential to consider the season and pack accordingly.

Spring (March to May):
Weather: Spring brings milder temperatures, ranging from 0 to 15°C (32 to 59°F). It's a transitional period with occasional rain.
Packing Tips: Pack layers, including a light jacket, waterproof shoes, and an umbrella for potential rain showers.

Summer (June to August):
Weather: Summers are pleasantly warm, averaging around 15 to 25°C (59 to 77°F). It's the best time for outdoor activities.
Packing Tips: Bring lightweight clothing, sunscreen, a hat, sunglasses, and comfortable shoes for exploring hiking trails and beaches.

Fall (September to November):
Weather: Fall temperatures range from 5 to 15°C (41 to 59°F). The island displays beautiful autumn foliage during this season.
Packing Tips: Pack layers, a warm jacket, and don't forget a camera to capture the vibrant fall colors.

Winter (December to February):
Weather: Winters are cold, with temperatures often below freezing. Snowfall is common, creating a winter wonderland.
Packing Tips: Bring a heavy winter coat, insulated boots, gloves, a hat, and layers to stay warm. If you plan on outdoor activities, consider packing snow gear.

General Tips:
Regardless of the season, it's wise to pack a travel-sized first aid kit, insect repellent, and any necessary medications.
Cape Breton's weather can be unpredictable, so it's advisable to check the forecast before your trip.
If you're planning outdoor adventures, such as hiking or kayaking, pack appropriate gear, including a sturdy pair of shoes, water bottles, and a backpack.
Remember to tailor your packing list based on the specific activities you plan to do and the season of your visit. Enjoy your trip to Cape Breton Island!

Safety Tips

Weather Awareness:
Check the weather forecast before your trip.
Pack accordingly for different weather conditions – bring layers, a rain jacket, and sunscreen.

Road Safety:
Follow speed limits and road signs.
Be cautious on winding roads, especially in rural areas.
Watch out for wildlife, like moose, on the roads.

Map and Navigation:
Carry a map or use a GPS to navigate.
Plan your route in advance and inform someone about your travel plans.

Emergency Contacts:
Save emergency contacts in your phone and write down local emergency numbers.
Know the location of the nearest hospital or medical facility.

Vehicle Maintenance:
Ensure your vehicle is in good condition before the journey.
Check tires, brakes, and fluids to avoid breakdowns.

Water Safety:
If near the water, be cautious of strong currents.
Follow safety guidelines if participating in water activities.

Wildlife Interaction:
Admire wildlife from a safe distance.
Do not approach or feed wild animals.

Trail Etiquette:
If hiking, stick to marked trails.
Carry enough water and snacks, and let someone know your hiking plans.

Local Regulations:
Familiarize yourself with local rules and regulations.
Respect the environment and local communities.

Health Precautions:
Pack any necessary medications.
Stay hydrated, especially if engaging in outdoor activities.

Cultural Sensitivity:
Be respectful of local customs and traditions.
Ask for permission before taking photos of people.

Stay Informed:
Stay updated on local news and conditions.
Know the location of your country's embassy or consulate.

Remember, safety is a priority, and being prepared enhances the enjoyment of your trip. Have a wonderful time exploring Cape Breton Island!

Useful Phrases

Greetings and Politeness:
Hello! How are you?
Good morning/afternoon/evening!
Thank you (very much)!
Excuse me, please.

Asking for Information:
Can you help me find [place]?
Where is the nearest [restaurant/hotel/market]?
What's the best way to get to [attraction]?

Navigating and Directions:
Is it far from here?
Which way to [destination]?
Can you show me on the map?

Ordering Food:
I'd like to order [dish].
Could I have [drink] please?
Is there a local specialty you recommend?

Shopping Phrases:
How much does this cost?
Can I get a discount?
Do you accept credit cards?

Emergencies:
Help! Call the police/ambulance!
I've lost my [item], have you seen it?
Is there a hospital nearby?

Weather Conversations:
What's the weather like today?
Is it going to rain tomorrow?
Do I need to bring a jacket?

Compliments and Expressions:
This place is beautiful!
The food is delicious.

I love the culture here.

Basic Local Phrases:
How do you say [common phrase] in Gaelic?
What's the local custom for [occasion]?

Farewells:
Goodbye!
See you later!
Thank you for your help.
Remember, people appreciate it when you make an effort to speak their language, even if it's just a few phrases. Enjoy your trip to Cape Breton Island!

Chapter 8: Local Events and Festivals

Annual Events Calendar

Whether you're a nature enthusiast, music lover, or history buff, there's something for everyone throughout the year.

January - March: Winter Wonderland
Embrace the winter magic with events like the Celtic Colours International Festival, showcasing traditional music and dance against a backdrop of snowy landscapes. Participate in outdoor activities like ice fishing or take in the breathtaking views along the Cabot Trail.

April - June: Spring Awakening
As spring unfolds, experience the Cabot Trail Relay Race, a team event that takes you through picturesque landscapes. Explore local farmers' markets, where you can savor fresh produce and handmade crafts. Don't miss the Cape Breton Bike Rally for a mix of scenic rides and camaraderie.

July - September: Festival Season
Summer brings an array of festivals, including the Cape Breton Music Festival, where you can immerse yourself in the soulful tunes of local musicians. Engage in ceilidh dances, traditional Gaelic gatherings, and the renowned Louisbourg Crab Fest, celebrating the island's seafood heritage.

October - December: Fall Foliage and Holiday Cheer
Witness the vibrant fall foliage along the Cabot Trail, creating a stunning backdrop for events like the Celtic Colours Artisan Market. As winter approaches, join the Christmas celebrations in towns like Baddeck, adorned with festive lights and local charm.

Throughout the year, you can explore historical sites such as the Fortress of Louisbourg and engage in outdoor activities like hiking, kayaking, and whale watching. Cape Breton's annual events calendar ensures a dynamic and culturally enriching experience for every traveler.

Participating in Festivals

The island, known for its vibrant cultural scene, hosts a variety of festivals throughout the year that showcase its rich heritage. One such event is the Celtic Colours International Festival, a celebration of Celtic music and culture.

Start your festival adventure by checking the event schedule in advance. The Celtic Colours Festival, typically held in October, features concerts, workshops, and community events across the island. Plan your visit to align with the festival dates, ensuring you don't miss the lively atmosphere and diverse performances.

Immerse yourself in the local culture by attending traditional music sessions. These informal gatherings often take place in local pubs and community centers, offering an intimate setting to enjoy the authentic sounds of Cape Breton's music scene. Don't hesitate to join in, as these sessions are known for their welcoming atmosphere, where locals and visitors come together to share a love for music.

Explore the local crafts and culinary delights at festival markets. Many events feature artisan markets showcasing handmade crafts, local artwork, and delicious food. Take your time strolling through these markets, interacting with local artists, and savoring the flavors of Cape Breton cuisine.

Consider participating in workshops and interactive sessions offered during the festivals. From traditional dance lessons to storytelling sessions, these activities provide hands-on experiences that deepen your connection to the island's culture. Engaging with local artists and experts can enhance your understanding of Cape Breton's unique traditions.

Take advantage of the festival's community events, which often include ceilidhs, a traditional Gaelic social gathering with music and dancing. Attendees of all ages join in the festivities, creating an inclusive environment that reflects the island's warm and friendly community spirit.

Lastly, don't forget to capture the moments. Whether through photographs, sketches, or simply journaling your experiences, documenting your festival journey allows you to relive the memories and share the magic of Cape Breton's festivals with others.

In summary, participating in festivals on Cape Breton Island involves immersing yourself in the local culture, enjoying traditional music sessions, exploring markets, joining workshops, and embracing the sense of community during events. It's a chance to create lasting memories while celebrating the vibrant spirit of this captivating island.

Community Celebrations

One of the standout events is the annual "Celtic Colours International Festival," a ten-day extravaganza showcasing the island's deep-rooted Celtic heritage.

As you meander through the charming villages and towns, you'll encounter lively ceilidhs, where the infectious rhythms of traditional music fill the air, and locals invite you to join in the spirited dances. The warm hospitality of the community is palpable, creating an atmosphere that instantly makes you feel like part of the extended Cape Breton family.

During the festival, be sure to explore the "Taste of the Cabot Trail," a culinary celebration that highlights the region's delectable seafood, hearty stews, and mouthwatering desserts. This gastronomic journey provides a delicious insight into the island's culinary traditions, fostering a sense of unity through shared meals and shared stories.

In the heart of Cape Breton, the "Gaelic College" hosts events throughout the year, offering a glimpse into the island's Gaelic heritage. From language workshops to traditional crafts, these gatherings create a sense of community pride, emphasizing the importance of preserving cultural practices for future generations.

As you traverse the island, you'll encounter smaller, yet equally spirited, community celebrations. Whether it's a local fiddling contest in Baddeck or a lobster festival in Ingonish, these events provide a window into the daily lives of Cape Bretoners and offer opportunities to connect with the friendly locals.

In the smaller communities, like Chéticamp or Mabou, the celebrations often revolve around seasonal traditions, such as summer street festivals or winter carnivals. These events not only showcase the resilience of the community but also underscore the importance of coming together to celebrate life's simple pleasures.

In essence, Cape Breton Island's community celebrations are a testament to the island's warm and inclusive spirit. From the grand scale of the Celtic Colours Festival to the intimate gatherings in charming villages, each event contributes to the vibrant mosaic of Cape Breton's cultural heritage, leaving a lasting impression on all who have the pleasure of partaking in these joyous occasions.

Chapter 9: Additional Tips

Sustainable Travel Practices

Here are some simple yet effective tips to make your travel eco-friendly:

Transportation:
Choose eco-friendly modes of transportation like electric or hybrid vehicles.
Opt for public transportation or carpooling to reduce individual carbon emissions.
Consider walking or cycling for short distances to explore the area sustainably.

Accommodation:
Select accommodations that prioritize sustainability, such as eco-friendly hotels or lodges.
Conserve energy by turning off lights and electronics when not in use.
Reuse towels and linens to minimize water and energy consumption.

Waste Reduction:
Carry a reusable water bottle and avoid single-use plastics.
Dispose of waste responsibly by recycling and using designated bins.
Minimize paper usage by opting for digital maps and guides.

Support Local Communities:
Choose locally-owned businesses for meals and souvenirs to contribute to the local economy.
Participate in community-based activities or tours to support sustainable tourism initiatives.

Wildlife Conservation:
Respect wildlife and observe from a distance, avoiding any disruptive behavior.
Choose tour operators committed to wildlife conservation and responsible practices.

Cultural Respect:
Learn about and respect the local customs and traditions of Cape Breton.
Support cultural heritage by visiting museums, art galleries, and local performances.

Nature Preservation:
Stay on designated trails and follow Leave No Trace principles to preserve natural habitats.
Avoid picking plants or disturbing wildlife to maintain the ecological balance.

Energy Conservation:
Conserve energy by turning off air conditioning and heating when not needed.

Use energy-efficient appliances and lighting in your accommodation.

Educate Yourself:
Prioritize destinations that promote sustainable tourism and environmental conservation.
Stay informed about the local environment and wildlife to make responsible choices.

Offset Carbon Footprint:
Consider carbon offset programs to compensate for the emissions generated during your travel.
By adopting these sustainable travel practices, you can enjoy your trip to Cape Breton Island while minimizing your environmental impact and contributing to the well-being of the destination.

Photography Tips

Here are some detailed photography tips for your travel to Cape Breton Island:

Golden Hours: Take advantage of the soft, warm light during sunrise and sunset. The "golden hours" provide a beautiful glow that enhances landscapes. Plan your shoots around these times for stunning results.

Scout Locations: Explore the island beforehand to identify key spots. Cape Breton is known for its rugged coastline, lush landscapes, and charming villages. Research popular viewpoints and hidden gems to capture a variety of scenes.

Weather Awareness: The island's weather can be unpredictable. Be prepared for sudden changes, and embrace the opportunity to capture dramatic cloud formations, misty mountains, or sun breaking through storm clouds.

Wide-Angle Lens: Bring a wide-angle lens to capture the vastness of the landscapes. This is especially useful for panoramic views of the coastline, expansive fields, and picturesque villages.

Long Exposures: Utilize long exposure techniques, especially when photographing waterfalls or coastal scenes. A slow shutter speed can create a smooth, dreamy effect for flowing water and capture the movement of waves.

Local Culture: Don't forget to include the local culture in your shots. Capture the unique architecture, traditional music, and friendly locals to tell a more comprehensive story of your Cape Breton experience.

Wildlife Photography: Cape Breton is home to diverse wildlife. Be patient and observant to capture birds, seals, or even moose. Use a telephoto lens for close-up shots without disturbing the animals.

Seasonal Changes: Consider the time of year for your visit. Cape Breton's landscapes transform with the seasons, from vibrant autumn foliage to snowy winter scenes. Each season offers unique photographic opportunities.

Composition Techniques: Apply basic composition principles like the rule of thirds, leading lines, and framing. These techniques can enhance the visual appeal of your photos and guide the viewer's eye through the image.

Storytelling: Tell a story through your photos. Create a narrative by capturing different aspects of your journey, from the scenic landscapes to the people you encounter. This will add depth to your photography collection.

Remember to enjoy the process and be open to spontaneous moments. Cape Breton's beauty is diverse, so embrace the unique character of each location you explore. Happy shooting!

Connecting with Locals

Start by exploring local cafes, markets, or community events, as these places often serve as hubs for locals. Engage in casual conversations by asking open-ended questions about the island, its culture, or their favorite spots.

Consider joining group activities or workshops, like local art classes or community gatherings. This provides a natural setting to meet people who share common interests. Be open to learning about their way of life and traditions, and don't hesitate to share a bit about yourself.

Attending local events, such as festivals or music performances, can be an excellent way to immerse yourself in the community spirit. Strike up conversations with fellow attendees, and don't be afraid to express your enthusiasm for the local culture.

Visiting smaller, family-owned businesses can also lead to meaningful connections. Chat with shopkeepers, artisans, or restaurant owners. They often have fascinating stories to share and can provide valuable insights into the local way of life.

If you're comfortable, consider using social media or travel forums to connect with locals in advance. Seek recommendations, ask for tips, and express your excitement about experiencing Cape Breton Island. Locals are often happy to share their favorite hidden gems and offer guidance.

Finally, be mindful of cultural nuances, show genuine interest, and be open to embracing the slower pace of life on the island. Remember that building connections takes time, so approach each interaction with patience and an eagerness to learn from the wonderful people of Cape Breton.

Appendix

Emergency Contacts

Local Emergency Services:
Police: Dial 911 for any urgent law enforcement assistance.
Fire Department: Call 911 in case of fires or other emergencies requiring firefighting services.
Medical Emergency: Dial 911 for immediate medical assistance.

Hospital and Medical Contacts:
Cape Breton Regional Hospital: In case of medical emergencies, contact the hospital at [insert hospital phone number].
Local Clinics: Know the contact details of nearby medical clinics for non-emergency healthcare needs.

Accommodation Contacts:
Your Accommodation: Keep the phone number of where you're staying handy, in case you need assistance or have an emergency at your accommodation.

Transportation Contacts:
Car Rental Company: Save the contact information for the company you rented your vehicle from.
Local Taxis or Rideshare Services: Note down the numbers of local taxi services or use apps for rideshare options.

Consulate or Embassy:
Embassy/Consulate Contacts: If you're from another country, have the contact details for your country's embassy or consulate in case of emergencies or lost documents.

Travel Insurance:
Insurance Provider: Keep your travel insurance information accessible. Note the contact number for emergencies and policy details.

Local Authorities and Information:
Tourist Information Center: Save the number for local tourist information centers for guidance on local services or attractions.
Local Police Station: Have the non-emergency police station contact for less urgent matters.

Personal Emergency Contacts:
Family and Friends: Share your travel itinerary and emergency contacts with family and friends back home.
Remember to program these numbers into your phone and have a written list as a backup. Stay safe and enjoy your trip to Cape Breton Island!

Made in the USA
Monee, IL
11 March 2024